ETERNAL LOVE

THE TRUE LOVE STORY OF NELLIE AND LOU MOORE

LOUIS MOORE

ISBN: 978-0-578-80937-3 (hc)

Library of Congress Control Number: 2020923266

This book is dedicated to my dearest wife/partner, Nellie,
who has given me 74 years of Eternal Love.

Nellie & Lou in the early 1990's

CHAPTER ONE

My story begins with my china doll wife, Nellie. I'm going to give you the facts so that you will understand her. People will say, "Why do you call this a story? A story is usually fiction, but this is not." These stories actually happened. I want all you dear readers to know dear Nellie.

Nellie was born in Fresno, on August 28, 1922. She was born of parents who came from Japan and were totally Japanese. They were in their early mid-life when they came to America to seek their fortune. They settled in Fresno, not knowing anything about America or the American people. Nellie's mother was very strong and very ambitious and learned the farming industries. Her parents moved to Visalia and Nellie graduated school and was a secretary of the graduating class. They went to school, she and her younger brother, and they worked the farm with their parents after school, weekends, holidays and vacation times. Her older sister tended the house— the cooking and cleaning and helping the family.

Nellie is a wonderful person who learned the farming industry the hard way. She showed me how to plant plants, tiny vegetables, and always made our home a very wonderful place.

Then, December 7, 1941 happened and the whole world collapsed. A war hungry general was put in charge of the west coast and he hated the Japanese and he wanted to declare war on them then. He convinced President Roosevelt that the Japanese were spies and needed to be put away. He built up concentration camps and put all the families into these camps. All the Japanese people were gathered up and put into the camps without any justice or jury. They were packed up and sent into the camps.

Nellie's family couldn't take anything with them, except what they could carry. They lost their farm, animals, trucks, and their home. The Japanese-

American citizens were even gathered up and sent to the camps too. The camps were surrounded with steel fencing 8-10 feet high. There were tall sentry boxes, armed with soldiers, with the rifles and bayonets. There was no trouble however. The people went meekly and broken-hearted. When this happened, all the white people grabbed the Japanese people's property, homes, furniture, etc.

Nellie's family went to camp and she endured it. Eventually, the war started to end and several and the families were told to go home, but Nellie didn't have a home to go to. In 1945, Nellie's parents told her to go to New York to get a job since the feelings towards the Japanese were so unkind on the west coast. She went to Larchmont, New York, where she took a job as a nanny.

I was born on October 30, 1922. Nellie and I are both the same age. We'll both be 98 years old this year, in 2020. We're only separated by two months. Nellie's birthday is August 28, 1922.

On April 1, 1946, I received my honorable discharge from the United States Air Force. I was excited to leave Fort Dix, New Jersey and as I headed towards the exit gates, I realized it was April Fool's Day, but I was afraid to ask if it was correct. I was so excited and scared that I almost ran all the way to Brooklyn where my family lived. I ran like hell. I was greeted by my mother, father, sister, and younger brother. Everyone was so happy to have me home. It was a miracle I was never hurt.

As we sat having dinner in the dining room, my mother said, "They're opening up a Chinese night club, called The China Doll Nightclub on west 47th street between 7th Avenue and Broadway. My mother was very fortunate to make reservations for their opening night. My father, mother, sister, and I went to the opening night and sat at the edge of the dance floor, looking at the stage. I couldn't wait for the show to start. I couldn't even remember what I ate! I was so nervous for the show to start. I couldn't breathe. The lights dimmed and the lights went up over the stage. Out from around the orchestra, 10 girls came out, five from each side and sat in front of the stage. I couldn't take my eyes off of one girl, third from the right. The show was wonderful and I wanted to be there without my parents. I wanted to do what men do—talk to the girls and hug them, which I hadn't done for four years.

I went back the following night. In came a huge man. He was 5'10" and 250 pounds. He seemed huge. He scared the hell out of me. He asked, "What do you want?" I told him I wanted to see the show. He noticed my honorable discharge pin and that changed is attitude towards me. He guided me into the bar and I had a full view of the stage, the orchestra and I saw the whole show all over again. I waited anxiously for the girls to come out after the show—except the one girl I wanted to see. The girl in the third chair from the right.

One of the girls came up to me and introduced herself as Lu Mae. She knew who I was because my sister was a professional singer and everyone knew about me, her brother. She asked if I'd like to dance and I thought, "Yes! Of course, I'd love to dance with you." She was a wonderful dancer and she said I was too. We danced until her next show. She asked if I would wait for her until after her next show. I nursed another drink, which was very expensive in the night club. I waited for her and she invited me to go get something to eat.

Restaurants in Manhattan were open all night long. We went to a Jewish deli and had the best pastrami in the world. We couldn't eat too much because she had to go back to do another show. We went back and she asked me to wait for her again. Again, I saw my girl, the girl that was seated third from the right in the chorus line.

I went back again the following day and watched the show again and again and again. I never did see the girl I really wanted to see come out after the show. One night, the girl I had been longing to meet, finally came out and introduced herself to me. "My name is Nellie Maeda." I never saw her again after that until June 1, 1946. One day she was in Hansen's luncheonette and I looked across the street from The China Doll and saw her sitting at the counter of the luncheonette having a cup of coffee. I became very excited and rushed across the street.

I said, "Hello, may I join you?" and she said yes. I ordered cups of coffee for us and we talked and talked. We enjoyed each other. I finally had my dream come true. As it was a few hours before her first show, we went on a walk together through Central Park. We walked into the park and found an empty bench. I dusted off the bench before she sat down and she was amazed that I would clean the bench for her. We talked and talked and talked. It was time to go back to the club and she asked if I would wait for her and of course I did.

June 1 was a very important date for us. On our second date, I began to feel feelings of expression and affection and I could feel the same from her. I pulled her close to me and kissed her. It was the first kiss of our lives together. I started to feel that I wanted to be with her forever. I could tell that she felt the same way too.

June 2, 3, 4, 5, 6, 7, 8, we met again and again together. I never saw the other girls from the show again. Every night we would meet, dance, get something to eat together and then enjoy each other.

June 9, we went to a Chinese restaurant and we sat opposite of each other. I asked if I could hold her hand and she gently extended her hand. I asked her if I could marry her. Her eyes started to fill with beautiful tears of love that were crystal clear. She said, "I want to be your wife too." We had a mutual feeling of love for each other that soon.

In New York, you had to wait several days between getting a license and getting married but Nellie and I didn't want to wait. In Baltimore, Maryland you didn't have to wait so we decided to not wait and to meet the next morning to take the train to Baltimore to get married. It was a six-hour ride from New York to Baltimore, we went directly to city hall, got our marriage license and headed to the Lord Baltimore Hotel. We went to the room and I went out to the gift shop and I bought one long stem rose. It was the first flower I ever bought for anyone. When she opened the door, I hid the rose behind my back. I had her close her eyes and then I put the rose in front of me and invited her to open her eyes. No one had ever given her a flower before and she was so happy. We went downstairs and asked if there was a nearby church where we could get married. We found a minister and his wife who performed the ceremony for us. When the minister said, "You are now man and wife," Nellie yelled out, "Oh my God, I am now Mrs. Nellie Moore!" She yelled it so loud, it shook Mount Rushmore! I always signed our names Nellie and Lou Moore. I always put her name her first.

We hailed a taxi driver and headed over to a nice restaurant. We went into the restaurant with a sawdust floor and checkered tablecloth. It was very cozy. We ended up walking back to the hotel, to our room and prepared ourselves for the evening.

Nellie & Lou at The Rainbow Room in New York City, on the occasion of their 1st anniversary.

We enjoyed each other with an act of love. We gave our bodies to each other in tenderness. We were the happiest couple in the whole world. We had a glorious wedding night of love and compassion. We don't like to use the word "sex." It's an act of tenderness, gentleness and togetherness. And so, we enjoyed the bliss of a wonderful wedding night and the 74 years that followed to this date in 2020.

The next day, back in New York, we went back to my mother's house. We were greeted by three people. My mother, father, and my sister. They were standing there with stern looks on their faces. They were angry and said, "Get out of here." They didn't like that I got married and didn't want me to marry a Japanese girl. We thought for sure my family would accept Nellie and accept our marriage. I felt so sorry for Nellie. We went to her apartment and lived there for a few months until we earned enough to move to California. When my family kicked us out, Nellie never said a word and never complained. She just took it.

Nellie called her sister up and told her that she married a Chinese man. Her sister refused to tell Nellie's mother, because her sister was scared.

We left for California and were met at the airport, by her sister and her sister's husband. They drove us to Little Tokyo. Her brother-in-law had a little jewelry store and they lived in a little apartment behind the jewelry store. I waited outside on a bench while Nellie talked with her sister. I was so afraid to meet my mother in law. Nellie was afraid her mother would raise holy heck for her marrying a Chinese man. Her sister and her husband lived behind a simple little jewelry store. Nothing fancy. Suddenly, in walked a woman 4'10", 90 lbs., storming in, walking in like a battle chief. She didn't even notice me. She was in talking with Nellie and her sister for quite a while before coming out to meet me. The three of them came out. Nellie, her sister, and her mother. She came out and looked at me, without expression. Her mother stared at me for the longest time. It felt like an eternity. Finally, her lips cracked open with a smile and she leaned forward to hug me. I couldn't believe it. She hugged me and I hugged her back for a long time. When we parted the hug, I could see she was crying. Tears of happiness and joy were flowing down her cheek. She accepted me and was pleased with me. I think the floor was flooded with tears. Not the greeting I got from my family. Nellie and her sisters started to bawl like hell. Her mother broke the ice with her acceptance of me. Later, a new chapter begins. Her mother treated me better than my mother ever treated me.

CHAPTER TWO

WE LIVED WITH NELLIE'S SISTER, BECAUSE THEY HAD room in the apartment. Jobs were scarce. I finally found a job in a Chinese restaurant on Ventura Blvd., just north of Hollywood and south of Studio City. It was owned by James Wong Howe, a famous Hollywood camera man. He was a tyrant. Whenever he came into the restaurant, he would bring friends and I always felt so badly for anyone that had to serve him. He won three academy awards. He was famous. I was excited that I had a job. I thought, I can't get from Little Tokyo to my job but Nellie tapped me on the shoulder and said, "Turn around and look across the street," and there was a string of Motels on Ventura Blvd. We went to one of the motels. She spoke with one of the managers and said, I will bring my own linen and wash my own linen if you'll give me a reduction and the owner agreed to reduce the rent. I walked across the street to and from work. I would always bring food from the restaurant for her to eat. Sometimes we would go to Studio City to window shop or shop. She made the motel room nice for the two of us. I made enough money on tips to buy a used car and we were able to find a house to rent.

Nellie's mother was so good to me. Whenever we visited her, she would always cook my favorite noodle dish for me. Her mother was wonderful. I think in the back of her mind, she accepted me more so later on because she realized I took good care of Nellie.

A funny memory that took place around 1950: My first experience with Nellie driving was during a trip we took to see some of my family in San Francisco. Nellie asked me if I would like her to drive for a while as I was getting tired. We switched placed but before I fell asleep, I told her, "Don't go over 70," and she smiled and said, "Oh sure!" I woke up and cracked one eye open and noticed she was driving 95 mile per hour. She was racing a train that was traveling in the same direction! I almost died! I told her to pull over so I could drive. Oh, she's such a wonderful person.

The restaurant closed up because of bad business practices of the owner. I found a job at a mom and pop grocery store. When I asked for a raise, I was fired. Nellie had an idea with the $20 we had left. Nellie had the idea to buy tubs full of fortune cookies, almond cakes, Chinese tea, and wax bags and a stapler. We bagged them and I sold them door-to-door for a couple of months. We were brave to do it. I sold the whole shebang within hours. After I did this for a couple of months, Nellie decided to join me. She always wanted to help. I would walk one side of the street and she would walk the other side. We did this for three months and made enough to pay for a car, our rent, and our utilities. This was Nellie's idea and it worked!

I finally got a regular job paying 95 cents an hour at a huge manufacturing plant. They made tv tuners. My job was to make sure the production line had enough material to work with. I had to make sure the warehouse supplied enough materials for the production line. I noticed that one of the managers always dressed impeccably and I decided to do the same because people seemed to respect him. He was promoted and recommended that I be promoted to his previous position. I received a pay promotion of $1.35/hour and we were elated. I was now a supervisor! Nellie said that I needed to dress the part of a supervisor. I was able to get her a job on the production line. It was very hard work, but she was willing to do it because she said, "It will help us." Her hands would get cut and would bleed from the difficulty of the work.

Nellie always had a bottle of scotch and a carton of cigarettes every night waiting for me. I smoked for the first 20 years of our marriage. I never gave any consideration to Nellie. She never complained about my smoking. Never. One day in 1969, something came out of my nose that scared me, so I stopped smoking. That's when I realized what I was doing to Nell while I was smoking. The carpets smelled, the drapes smelled. The dogs smelled. I just didn't realize it. I apologized to Nell. I apologized almost every day to Nell. I realized how terrible it is on people who don't smoke.

Nellie always thought of me first, before she ever thought of herself. I was promoted and able to buy nice clothes, eat out at restaurants, and give her mother money. This was all possible because Nellie saw that motel.

I was able to go to a management dinner, when the owner gave us 30% of our annual salary. This was at a fancy Christmas party at the Sheraton hotel. All the managers and their wives were invited. Nell took care of our finances. Every nickel I ever made, Nellie managed. She took care of all the bills. She took care of everything. She did it all and she never made a mistake. Our credit rating was 916 because of her. I always let her know how happy I was that she took care of our finances; how happy I am to be her husband. Without WW2 we would never have met.

Eventually, something nice happened and I will entitle it Mr. Mo Grudd. In the 1950's, Nellie worked as a hostess at a Chinese restaurant near Studio City, in North Hollywood. Being the type of person she is, (so congenial, so nice, always a smile on her face) all customers liked her. One customer took a liking to her. His name was Mr. Grudd. He was an attorney and about 65 years old and 5'10". He was rotund. He loved to eat and he took to Nellie. It was a blessing. I never met him but Nellie told me about him. One weekend, he asked Nellie if he could take us to dinner as his guest. He was a Hollywood lawyer.

Many of his clients were in tv and the movies. We agreed to go, and he took us to a very nice restaurant in the Hollywood hills named, The Bull. The restaurant was something very English. We felt out of our element eating there.

From that point on, Mr. Mo Grudd took us to baseball and basketball games, the Ice Capades and many live stage shows. All he asked from us was our friendship and company. We became very, very good friends. This brought us to another phase in our lives.

In early 1959, Nellie said to me, "It's about time we bought a home." I agreed because we now had the money to buy one. So, we went looking. It took a while to find something Nellie liked. We drove around and wound up in Woodland Hills. To the north of Ventura Blvd., there was a new development going up. They were all very classy homes. We thought, "It's out of our league." Nell and I walked into the managers model apartment in one of the homes. It was difficult because people would exclude Asians from owning homes, property, stores, etc. Nell loved the home, so we took our chances. After inspecting the literature we brought home, we decided to talk with Mr. Grudd to see if he could help us. One day, while out to dinner together, we approached him about this home on Carlton Terrace. I told him about our concern that we would be excluded from buying property because we were Asian. He offered to buy the home and then sell it to us. Nellie showed him all the details of everything she wanted. I agreed to pay him every cent of everything he had to pay for. All of this because of Nellie and her wonderful personality. Nellie was elated because she was going to get her home.

The home was 2000 square feet, three bedrooms, two bathrooms with a huge hill behind the house. It was her castle. Once Mr. Grudd closed on the house, he kept his word and sold the house to us. It was so amazing that a person would do this for us! The deal was sealed with a handshake. Shortly, about three months after we got the house, Mr. Grudd passed away from a heart attack. (I don't like to use the phrase, "he died." When someone is very close to you, I think it's better to say "passed away." "Died" is for someone who isn't close to you.)

Not long after we moved in, a petition went around the neighborhood, wanting us to leave. They didn't want us to live among them. Most of the neighbors had three mortgages and couldn't even keep their home, but we were able to maintain and live in our home. Nellie made it beautiful; she always made it beautiful. I never questioned her about anything she ever wanted. I never had to question her because she was very practical.

We were living in our home that Mr. Grudd bought. Nellie went out for a little bit to get gas and when she came back and said that she had met the Academy Award winning actor, Mr. Ernest Borgnine. Nellie and Mr. Borgnine became very good friends. They met every weekend when Nellie went to fill up the gas tank. She said that Mr. Borgnine invited us to his home for Christmas dinner and said that he wanted the two of us to come to his home so we did. How often do you get invited to a movie star's house? We hesitated about going because we wondered, "Why would he invite us?"

We went 45 minutes to an hour late. We went like we were dressed up for church. He answered his door wearing a flannel shirt, jeans and boots, with a scowl on his face. He said, "Where the hell have you been?" He brought us to the dinning room with 12 people, who were also dressed casually, and two empty chairs. We thought this would be a party for many, many people! From that day one, he would always send us flowers and candy. For any occasion, he would always send us a huge chocolates and flowers, no matter where in the country he was.

In 2000, Mr. Borgnine invited us to his book signing in Pasadena. He sent a limousine for us and brought us to a beautiful restaurant. As we arrived, he greeted us with hugs. He had one of his books that he had inscribed. We had a wonderful dinner. Afterwards, we went to his book signing. Inside and outside of the bookstore was a line, a mile long. He had us stay by his side while he signed the books. He was so wonderful to each person who came to have him sign their book. A few years later, he passed away.

Nellie & Ernest Borgnine at Nellie & Lou's 50th wedding anniversary celebration.

We knew him from 1959 – 2010. We knew him all those years. He was a dear, dear friend. I don't know that Nellie cried harder for anybody else.

Eventually we ended up in the state of Washington. We were lured up there by someone we thought was a very good friend, Jane Powell's father, (Jane was an American movie star). At least we thought Mr. Powell was a very good friend. He kept urging us to come up there and kept after us because he knew what we could do to help get his café going. Things were not going well with the economy in Los Angeles, so we thought we'd take a chance and moved to Longview, Washington. As usual with partnerships, when it comes to money, true character comes out. He was quickly the "boss" and we were no longer friends.

We had moved up there and Nellie thought it would be a good idea to open a Chinese restaurant. She suggested the name, "The Gold Lantern". I said, "Who's going to do the cooking?" and Nellie pointed at me. I had never cooked for a large group of people, but Nellie assured me that she would help me. The name was Nellie's idea. As it got closer to the opening date, I got sick. I was so nervous. I went to a restaurant near Portland that we frequently went to and asked to see their kitchen. I looked at the huge woks, and how hard they were working, doing all the cooking, and I felt lost! There was no way I could do that.

We had hired help and had everything ready to go with the restaurant. I rewarded all the people who had come to help and I made a feast of a dinner for them. There were no Orientals. They were all white, young people and they were totally enjoying themselves. I was getting sicker and sicker.

Finally, we opened and Nellie put the recipe of each dinner we served on a spinner. Our first night turned out all right. Eventually, I became a great chef. The same customers would come twice a week. My cooking became the talk of the town. Before we opened the restaurant, we told Mr. Borgnine that we were opening the restaurant. He gave us a signed picture and we it up in the restaurant but nobody believed he gave it to us. Then, the most fabulous thing about the restaurant was when our friend Ernie Borgnine (Emperor of the North) came to the restaurant during a three-day holiday. He brought his girlfriend and came to show the town that he knew us. He came and we drove him around touring the city so they could see we really knew him. He won the 1954 Academy Award for the movie, "Marty".

One day in the restaurant a customer wanted some dessert but we said we didn't have any. Nellie decided to bake a pie for the customers. They loved it! Word spread about how good the pie was! They came to eat the pie instead of the Chinese food! She was always full of surprises. She became the Marie Callender's of the north.

One night I felt so good about the help and the restaurant, I cooked a special dish for the help, called Tomato Beef. All the help loved it. The next night, each waitress came in and ordered "Tomato Beef," "Tomato Beef." They were suggesting it to the customers. I was worried that I wouldn't have enough tomatoes. The next night a young man came to the restaurant, who was dressed rather sloppily. He ate it an exclaimed, "This is the best tomato beef. It's even better than my mother's!" The next week he came again, dressed up like he was going to church, and he brought in his entire family to try my tomato beef.

One day, when I was on my way to get supplies from Portland, Oregon, I was t-boned by a man who was drunk. I was laid up for 6 months in traction. Because of my accident, we lost the café. We next moved to Pasco, Washington because I had a job. Nellie took a job as a bookkeeper. The owner of the agency loved her and was very satisfied with the job she did. I took odd jobs too, but we didn't see any future in staying up there. We both decided it was time to go back to Los Angeles. I told Nellie she should go first so she could find a job that could support us and I could find a job that aligned with my career.

CHAPTER THREE

NELLIE WAS A GREAT LOVER OF SMALL ANIMALS. WE lived in an apartment by a huge lake. The lake was surrounded by apartments. It was a beautiful place. Nellie would go out and would feed the ducks. She went out and bought sacks of grain. We had a deck that would lead from our living room to the lake. Nellie would leave a trail of grain from the deck to the lake if she couldn't stay out to feed. The ducks eventually made a nest right under our window. Even the animals loved Nellie! One of the ducks became hurt and Nellie would care for it and take care of it. That duck became her duck and Nellie named him Louie.

We had three dogs, all wire-haired terriers. They were not too big and not too small. One of the dogs loved Nellie SO much he wouldn't let me in the house when I'd come home from work. The dog that was the most precious to Nellie was a dog named Corky. That dog was with Nellie 24 hours a day. Everything that dog learned was from Nellie. At night, Nellie would give her three little biscuits and she would take them to her bed. Somehow Nellie taught our dog Corky how to count. One night, Nellie only gave Corky 2 biscuits, but she wouldn't stop looking at Nellie until she gave her the third biscuit. Corky was SO smart. That dog LOVED Nellie. Sometimes I would tease that I was going to hit Nellie just to see what she would do, and Corky would show her teeth and growl. She was very, very protective of Nellie and very precious to her.

Before we moved to the Antelope Valley, we lived in Los Feliz. There were squirrels all over the place near our apartment. Nell loved the squirrels and would buy sacks of peanuts to feed the squirrels. We spent more money on peanuts than we did on bread! One day, when Nellie was sitting on the wall resting, the squirrel came up to her and looked at her until Nellie gave it a peanut. Before you knew it, the squirrel was sitting on the wall, next to Nellie while she fed it. Eventually I came down from the apartment and I saw the squirrel sitting in Nellie's lap! She got that squirrel to trust her!

Nellie and her squirrel in the late 1990s.

One day, a few years later, I came down early before Nell, to feed the squirrels. Finally, I saw the squirrel in the bushes next to the apartment. It must've been hit by a car.

I could see the squirrel partially in the bushes. I tossed a peanut and the squirrel didn't move at all. I called for Nellie and she came down and called to the squirrel. She came out long enough to eat a peanut from Nell, and then went into the bushes to die. She lived long enough to see Nellie one last time.

When we were living in Washington, we felt we should come back to LA to be near her family. I told Nell, she should go first and find a job. I needed to find a job that fit my career. She came down first to LA and her sister-in-law helped her to find an apartment in Los Feliz, where we lived for 35 years. Nellie was able to get a job at an engineering company. Everybody was white and Nellie was the only Asian in the entire company. Nellie worked there for several years before the company closed. The same man who helped her get the job, helped her to get another job in an engineering company in Van Nuys. Nellie was a helper to the director of Human Resources. Nellie was doing everything while the director was doing nothing. Eventually, the woman left the company and the President of the company asked Nellie to be the director of Human Resources. Nellie was flabbergasted! Nellie told the owner that the salary he offered was not enough. I had taught her how business works so she knew how to advocate for herself. She was tickled pink. Nellie did a fabulous job for the company. Nellie was a wonderful office person. She knew how to organize at work, just like she did at home. She worked in that position until 1988, when she retired. (I retired in 1987.) She moved up from nothing, all the way to the director. She knew her job so well.

We traveled to many, many places after we retired. I had a consulting business. I went to Japan for one of my companies and she was so happy to go with me. She was so thrilled to go to the small town of her mother's relatives. She was SO excited. While I was working, she was having a good time with her relatives. When she came back from being with her relatives, she told me that she went to the bathhouses with her family! I couldn't believe it!!!

When we came home, we bought Nellie a new car. We bought her a beautiful Buick Riviera. We traveled and traveled and traveled. Eventually we became adult tutors and taught people how to read. We registered with Glendale College and went on to teach English as a Second Language. It wasn't really Nellie's cup of tea, but it was mine. I volunteered for 12 years. In 1997, I was given an award for being the #1 tutor in English as a Second Language in the State of California. I always had 20-25 students every time I taught. I taught them how to live in America and how not to be cheated. I never want them to be cheated.

Nellie began to volunteer in the gift shop in a local hospital. She did a wonderful job organizing and helping people to find where they needed to go. Nellie gave people a feeling of hope. She did that for 18 years.

When I first met Nell in 1946, I took her out bowling. I asked her if she had ever bowled before and I told her I would show her what to do. Nellie bowled a 200 game the very first time! She told me she never bowled before. I was shocked. There were so many things she has done.

She gave me my first birthday party ever. Whenever someone would move into our neighborhood, she would bake a pie, or a cake or whatever to welcome new neighbors to our community. The gifts Nellie gave me from June 1 through June 9, 1946, one item was a Dunhill gold plated cigarette lighter. The other was a Remington Electric Razor. That was the first electric razor in those days. She took her salary and spent a lot of money on me. I don't know she did it. She worked and had rehearsals. I'm not sure how she found time to buy those gifts. She did it because she loved me. I was flabbergasted.

Nellie always encouraged me to do whatever I wanted to do. She never said, don't do it. She would always tell me, "You can do it. You can do it." There were so many projects that I wanted to do.

We never communicated or talked to my family for 7 years. One night, I said, "Do you know it's been 7 years since I've had contact with my family?" Nellie told me that I should call them. I called my family and we apologized to each other, but my apology was only half-hearted. My mother waited for me to apologize first. That says a lot about the kind of person she was. My mother felt it was my responsibility to apologize to her and take responsibility for what happened in 1946. I did apologize, or else she would never have accepted us back. She was never nice or cordial to Nellie.

My mother came out to visit and Nellie was so good to them, even though her heart was only half into it because of how my mother treated me. Nellie treated her very well. We picked her up from the airport. In the morning, my mother asked if we had fruit cocktail for breakfast. Then she asked for Sanka coffee. I went to the store and bought fruit cocktail for her to eat each morning, but she wouldn't eat it. We bought her Sanka coffee because it was the only coffee she would drink. But she wouldn't drink it. She was being rude to us. My mother was a pistol. The worst pistol you could imagine. You would not want her to be your enemy.

The reason we became comfortable was during the time of President Ronald Reagan. The interest rate went up to 18%. Nellie went out and bought annuities. I didn't think about it, but Nellie knew what to do. I always trusted her with our money.

There was an event that happened in the San Fernando Valley that used to happen every weekend. In the supermarket parking lots, artists would have these painting sales. Nellie painted watercolor paintings. She saw a certain lady and saw her paint. Nell bought one and kept buying her paintings. She must've bought 7 or 8 paintings. Nellie and this artist became friends. This artist invited us to her home and we had dinner. This woman was the 1941 Miss America, Rosemary LaPlanche. She would always give parties for us. One of the things Rosemary did was she made smoked salmon for me. I hate fish but she did it for me because she knew we had lived in Washington State. That's another friend that Nelly made.

One time when we were shopping in Nordstrom's in Glendale. We had separated in the department store. All of the sudden, Nellie came running up to me and said, "Come, come, come." Nordstrom had a small section for jewelry. She pointed out a beautiful chain necklace. Beautiful white and green. She said, "Isn't this beautiful?" Nellie wanted that necklace which was a beautiful piece of jade, so we bought it for her. I always supported her because I knew she would never choose anything that would put us in the poor house. I loved to buy her things that she loved.

When we were married, I could not afford a diamond ring. I bought her a zircon. In her later years, she wanted a diamond ring. Without telling me, she and her sister picked out a diamond ring. She called me at the office and asked if she could buy a diamond ring, a ring she had always wanted. A

1 carat, grade G. That's all the jewelry I ever bought her. All the rest, she bought herself.

Nellie had a flock of cousins in Washington DC. One relative worked at the Pentagon. We visited one year and unbeknownst to me, Nellie took her jewelry and gave pieces to each of her relatives. That's the way she thinks; she's very, very generous. She always shares with others. We had some family members who got married and had nothing! Nell went around our home and gathered up all kinds of things they could need and gave it to them. Another time, a family lost their home to a fire and Nellie did the same thing! She gathered everything she could from our house and gave it to them. We didn't even know these people. That's what Nellie did. She has the most fabulous heart.

Nellie, in her previous years has done many things to make people happy and to me one of the things that she did has to be told. In our apartment building in Los Feliz, there were three floors of five apartments each. We lived on the 2nd floor near an elderly woman, about 85 years old. During this time, Nellie and I were in our early 60's and working. Nellie became friendly with this woman. One evening, we arrived home at the same time, and

Nellie rushed into the apartment, dropped her purse and her coat and got some fancy cookies and fancy Chinese tea. She left with the items and went to visit this woman. She was gone for almost an hour. Mind you, she just got home from work. We hadn't had dinner, but this had to be done first. I understood it. To understand Nellie further, you have to know that Nellie visited this woman for about an hour each evening. She did this for a couple of years before this woman passed away. Nellie enjoyed helping her feel alive, as we all do with friends. In fact, Nellie said, "we should take her out to dinner once in a while," and this woman was very elated. She was a Caucasian woman and here were two Asian people caring for her and demonstrating their care. That woman was so happy with Nellie. Because she was so happy with Nellie, she bought me a Waterford Crystal whiskey glass! I'm not sure why she did that for me. Maybe because I never complained. That demonstrates the humanity in Nellie. To heck with my dinner; this woman's needs came first and I admired Nellie all the more because of what she was doing for this woman.

CHAPTER FOUR

WE FOUND AN APARTMENT WE LOVED IN LOS FELIZ.
Nellie found a job working for a
manufacturing/engineering company that built
kitchens for restaurants. I found a job with a good
company named, Pacific Mercury. They were in the
engineering field and they did a lot of work for the
aircraft industry. I started out as a buyer and was
then put into a team of engineers to develop Thomas
Electronic Organ. I was the buyer to find all the
materials they needed. I was able to find the
keyboard needed for the organ. Sometimes I had to
go out of the country to find the needed
components, including going to Japan. I was proud
of the work we did there.

Nellie found a great job and did very well with it. She was scared but I told her I would help her. I taught her how to respond in a business environment. After Pacific Mercury, someone that worked there and left for another company (the purchasing agent for an engineering firm,) recommended I take his place. He thought I would do a great job to oversee the whole process. Nellie in her true manner, helped me to help us to have a good life.

They tell me that I was born October 30, 1922. How I was born is very significant. My father, mother, and sister lived in Port Huron, Michigan. My father owned a few restaurants there. They returned to San Francisco and my mother gave birth to me there. They left me with me grandmother. For 4-5 years, I believed that my grandmother was my mother and that her sister, my aunt, was my second mother! When I was 4-5 years old, my parents came back to San Francisco to take me away. It was horrible. The most horrible moment of my life, because I didn't know them. They were strangers to me. They took me away from my grandmother and took me to a poor neighborhood in New York. When it was time to leave, I cried and hugged and wouldn't let go because I didn't want to leave my grandmother.

We ended up poor in New York because my father was a very stubborn man. He would get mad at his partners and just leave his businesses, without protecting his interests. We lived in a not very nice area near the Brooklyn Bridge. We finally moved into a very nice home in Flatbush and my mother sent for her mother and other family members to come and live with us. I think eventually we had 5 families living in that house! I was fine with it and considered them all my parents.

My sister was the jewel of the family. They all loved her. As I recall, they did not show love to me. My mother made me do everything in the house, including cleaning the bathrooms, cleaning the floors, etc. I felt like I was a slave and adopted. I didn't feel love from them. Everyone called me Junior. No one called me Lou.

When I was in grade school, my parents worked in a restaurant. They would leave messages for me to cook various items, until one day when I came home and the note said, "Cook the fish." My sister and uncle didn't like fish and neither did I and they said,

"Cook something else." My parents were so angry that I didn't cook the fish. "Why didn't you cook the fish?" (I didn't blame my sister or my uncle). My mother made me sit at the table while she cooked the fish and then she forced me to eat it. There was no water or milk or anything to go with the fish. I finished the fish and I swore at that moment I would never eat fish again. I hated it. My sister and my uncle never accepted any responsibility for it. I would often get slapped and beat. That was my life. Every time my sister cried, I got beat.

I loved going to school and I loved American History. Eventually I went to high school. My sister got an allowance but I had to earn mine. My father got me a job at a chop suey joint. I would wait on about 30-40 tables a day and would get about $5. When I graduated high school, my parents did not attend the ceremony. This assured me more than ever that I wasn't one of the family. I was an outsider.

Because of the conditions of the war in Europe, many jobs in manufacturing were available. I got a job at a company making good money. I never saw the paycheck. It went from me to her. Finally, my mother was happy with me.

I wanted to be a pilot, so I registered to take a test to become an aviation pilot for the army. The test was held at Grand Central Station. It was a HUGE room, filled with 200 other men taking the test. The test took two hours. The two sergeants stood up and said, if we call your name go to this side of the room. Eventually it came down to only 35 individuals still seated. He said if you're standing against the wall you can go. If you're seated, you passed. I was one of those still seated. I was so elated, I don't even remember how I reacted. I was tickled pink I guess. My mother FINALLY declared her love for me. She was finally proud of me.

I went down to Texas to be trained as a pilot for the army. During the course of my training. I had an accident. I flew an open cockpit ship. You sat on your parachute. One day the parachute was so uncomfortable so I moved my body and adjusted the parachute which impaired the controls and I crashed the plane. I was washed-out. I was so disappointed. I later learned that the class I graduated with were all killed in WWII, and I would've been one of them if that happened. I was lucky.

During WWII, I was stationed in France near the border to Germany. The war was beginning to lighten up. I received a pass to go to one of the small villages that surrounded a small portion of France, (they were called bistros). I sat at the outside table at this bistro, enjoying my drink. After my drink, my hand reached into my pocket, and I pulled out a new pack of cigarettes. When I did this, a middle-aged French man saw me bring out this package. I lit up the cigarette and put it too my lips. He was drooling. I offered a cigarette to him and he came and joined me at my table. Then he asked me for one for his wife, his son, his mother, mother-in-law, etc. It ended up being 19 people! He drained my package. It was a good thing he didn't have 20 family members. I was satisfied to see them happy. They loved American cigarettes. Oh well, it was only cigarettes!

Eventually I got a job at Standard Coil products—a huge manufacturing company. They provided products to make TVs. I got a job in the stock room at .95/hr. I was tickled pink with that. It was a huge stockroom. There were thousands of women working to make TV tuners. We had to make sure there were supplies for the production line to make all the tuners. The other stockroom boys would horse around because they were younger. The manager of the stockroom always dressed nicely. I watched every move he made and copied everything he did in my mind. Maybe I was hoping to have his job. When he left for a promotion, he recommended me to take his place as the manager/supervisor of the stockroom. When I told Nell, we hugged and kissed and danced because this meant a large increase in our income. Nellie told me we needed to go shopping for white shirts, ties, nice slacks so I could look the part too.

After a while, Nellie started wondering what she could do instead of being home alone all day at the home we were renting in North Hollywood. She thought maybe she could get a job in the production line at Standard Coil, but it was very difficult for her. It was a very hard job to fit about 100 components into a very small box and solder the pieces.

During this time, Nellie would occasionally make BBQ ribs. Her sauce was her own recipe and there was none other in the market like it. She made it every so often for us. One night when she had made it, we looked at each other and almost had the same idea. We said, "We like it. Do you think the public would like it? Why don't we try it!" We agreed on a plan. We would occasionally invite others over to dinner and serve them the BBQ sauce. We would ask them if they liked it and they would always say, "Yes, where can we get it?" I would say, "You can't. It's Nellie's private recipe." It was like our own focus groups.

Our next step was to put the sauce into jars and we had labels printed up. I took those jars to Standard Coil to get a sense if people would like it. It sold out instantly. It went like mad. A few days later, I questioned each person who bought the Chinese Sparerib sauce. They said, I didn't try it on spareribs. I tried it on fish, or chicken, or a host of other things. We decided to change the name by getting rid of the name Chinese Sparerib Sauce and just called it Nellie's BBQ Sauce. We were eventually able to place the sauce in Safeway, Ralph's, and some other specialty food stores. Unfortunately, we lost our shelf space and I didn't have the money for a marketing campaign, so we had to let the idea go. It would've taken too much money. We did find out that Nellie makes a damn good sauce!

I eventually was promoted to be one of the managers of the company. It was a very strategic position. The president gave a Christmas party every year for all the managers and their wives. He had the party one year at a beautiful hotel on the edge of Pasadena. We were so excited to attend. The bonus check we received was 30% of the annual salary, more money than we had seen and we were so excited. The President announced all of the names and called each manager up and handed them their check. I didn't open up the envelope but walked back to the table and handed the check to Nellie. The other men said, "Don't do that! Don't give that check to your wife!" But we always shared everything. In the meantime, Nellie got a job at a nice restaurant near Universal City. She met lots of movie industry people.

My life began after I met Nell. I worked my way up the ladder with different companies. I became adept at being a manager. More companies heard about me and wanted me to be manager for their new companies. Nellie always encouraged me saying, "You can do it. You can do it." It was wonderful!!!

CHAPTER FIVE

BACK IN THE 60S, NELLIE MET A JAPANESE FAMILY WHO
lived in the same area and became friends with
them. They were part of the Hollywood Chapter of a
Japanese-American Alliance for the under-
privileged, a national group. Nell wanted to go and
dragged me with her. We were sitting there in the
audience and a question came up and no one had
the answer. All of the sudden I felt a sharp elbow
from Nellie telling me to get up and say something. I
got up and gave my answer, which they all accepted.
This happened regularly until I almost had a dent in
my side. I provided many responses and they
eventually asked me to become a member of the
chapter. John Ball, the author of "In the Heat of the
Night" was a member of the group. We

became members and attended the meetings, both of us, even though I was Chinese-American and not Japanese. Eventually the time came when they were looking for new leadership and I was selected as the new president. I served as president for two years and then I felt someone else should have an opportunity. After that, Nellie would touch my lap gently with love when she thought I should say something. I was inaugurated at The Statler Hotel in Los Angeles. That was all because of Nellie's trust in me and always poking me in the ribs.

Although neither Nellie nor I are not fans of a rodeo, we went to one at the Rose Bowl in Pasadena. The only reason we went was because Ronald Reagan was the Grand Marshall and he was running for the Governor of California. We got our seats and sat down about 20 steps from the stadium field. On the row in front of us and a couple of seats to the right was a woman I recognized. I nudged Nell and said, "Look, there's Nancy Reagan!" There was no one else seated in the section. Ronald Reagan came riding by in in his white cowboy outfit and stopped to acknowledge his wife. Instinctively, I jumped up and yelled, "Here's is the next Governor of California!" Mr. Reagan said, thank you and Mrs. Reagan yelled with joy. We made small talk and next thing I knew, one of her aides brought me a brown bag filled with political item, pins, buttons, etc. for his political campaign. Nell and I enjoyed our one and only rodeo! What a coincidence to be sitting behind her. How we got those seats, I'll never know.

Each evening, after our dinner, I would always say, "That was a nice dinner." Nellie appreciated that. I meant it. I didn't say it for the sake of saying it. It came from my heart. As the years progressed, our love grew. We were in love for 74 years. Even after 74 years, we still greeted each other with a kiss and an "I love you." That's what made life so wonderful. We never tired of each other and never tired of holding hands or being together. We would watch tv together in the evening with our feet up on the table and holding hands. Nellie always encouraged me to be strong and take a new job.

I became well known in Longview, Washington. A friend in the city government asked me if I would be the director of fund raising for a local initiative for the American Heart Association. I organized it so well with people raising money and organizing where the workers would go to raise money. I got a notice from the City of Seattle inviting me to come and celebrate and received an award. We sat in a huge room with people who had worked as a fund raiser. They called my name up, but first said, "For the person who had the highest percentage increase of the past years for fundraising...Louis Moore." (Moore was the name given by immigration because they couldn't understand the Chinese last name.)

I was previously asked to be a vice president of a manufacturing firm and I said that I would need to meet the people who would be working for me. I asked if we could meet at The Velvet Turtle. I saw a man and woman come into the bar multiple times, walk in and walk out. They didn't realize I was Mr. Moore. They almost walked out until I introduced myself and suggested I buy them a drink. I was given the job and I said that I wanted to interview the department heads of the each of department they had. I got to the sales manager and asked, "How do you get your business?" He said, "People call us." I kept asking and finally asked, "What do you do when the phone doesn't ring?" I told the owner I would take the job but I wanted a specific amount of money and I wanted a contract. The owner said, "We don't have a contract, "and I said, "I'll dictate a contract. Get me your secretary!" I was very business-like. I got the job and I got the contract. I told the owner I would like to have a company car. She offered me a Cadillac so I had my first Cadillac —a company car.

During the course of running a company. I had a lot of educating to do with the people. They had no brains! One of the tanks we put up, the owner of the building came in one day yelling, saying, "The tank is overflowing with dust. It's not working." I sent my engineer over there and then I went over there. I'm not an engineer nor did I go to college, but I was able to see what was happening. They had made the opening too small and the dust was getting backed up. The tank funneled at the bottom and emptied into a truck. I was able to resolve the issue and I'm not an engineer!

There was another incident where I showed my brains. I would read the government's specifications so I always knew what I was talking about. I did my homework. There are more ignorant people in jobs they shouldn't have. You have to read and you have to understand what you read! By reading, I was able to outshine engineers!

After Thomas Electric, I went to work with a Japanese company, as a consultant. After the owner watched me for a time, the owner asked me to go to Japan to see if there were any other products the company could use. I called Nellie up and told her that I had to go to Japan for two weeks. At first, she wasn't too excited, until I invited her to come with me. She was TICKLED PINK. Then I could hear scream on the other side of the phone. She yelled, "I'm going to Japan," and all the women who worked with her screamed too. She was able to meet her mother's relatives she had never met before. Nellie was able to tour all around Japan on her own while I was working. She met so many family members and even took a public bath with her relatives.

During that trip, the companies that were entertaining me would take me to restaurants and have me eat raw fish, raw shrimp. One time, I could have sworn that a fish they were cutting up winked at me! I used so much soy sauce to kill the taste! All the companies thought they were doing me a favor taking me to the best fish places in town. Our very first meal in Japan, the host took us to a spaghetti house!

When I made business calls, the secretary would always ask, "May I ask who's calling?" and I would always say, "Yes you may." One day I heard a loud, "There's a Mr. Yes You May on the phone."

That's what I did. I was a management consultant for a long time. I retired in 1987, and Nellie retired in 1988.

Nellie and Lou together in Hawaii around 1984.

Our life was wonderful. We traveled a lot. We went to Las Vegas one time. She went her way and I went mine. I went to the Blackjack table. On the back of my seat was an aisle and then slot machines. I noticed the dealer kept looking up over my shoulder and smiling. He said, "Look!" I saw a gorgeous Oriental girl playing the slot machines. He said, "She's very smart. Look, she's wearing gloves (because in that day there was lead in the slot machine coins." I said, "hold a place for me," and walked over, lifted her head up and gave her a kiss. He said, "How did you do that?" I said, "Easy. That's my wife!" That was our life. We were always together. We went to the cleaners together. We went shopping together and we were always together. That's how everyone knew us. Together. We never had children because when you have children, the marriage ends. I always felt that Nellie would just be isolated with the children. We tried, and finally stopped trying to have a baby and enjoy each other. Nellie's love, devotion and confidence made me the person I became.

When we were living in our first home, it became too big for us. Nellie said, "We should get something smaller." She found a house that was smaller—very nice, and well built. It was the home of a building contractor and it was so well built. We had a lot of work to do because it was old. We re-painted each room. One night, she was painting in the living room and then I heard her scream. I ran into the room and there she was on the 5-ft. ladder, covered in paint, like syrup over ice cream. I don't know how I did it, but I got her into the car, into our other home and got her all cleaned up.

We loved that home. We re-did the entire kitchen and made it stainless steel kitchen. When we were in one of the businesses to purchase the new items, it was clear that the salesman didn't respect Orientals. I said that we wanted to buy a number of items, spending money and he was in for a shock.

My mother and father came to visit us in Los Angeles. I took them to China Town for dinner. When they would go out of town, my mother would buy useless things, just to see my father cry. We went to Chinese gift store and my mother filled a table with all of the items she had picked to purchase. She picked another item without a price and the salesman went to ask the boss. The Japanese boss said in Japanese, "Oh, they're Chinese tourists. Charge them double the price." Nellie whispered it to me. Nellie heard everything word he said. I told the owner, "My wife is Japanese and she heard every word you said. We won't buy any of these things!" It was about $500 worth of goods. That's just another example of something wonderful that Nellie did. As we walked out of the shop, I gave Nellie a lovingly tender pat on her rear end as I whispered in her ear, "I love you."

Nellie has done so much to influence my life. We have influenced each other. Both of us are a couple that I wish the whole world was like. In a marriage, you are partners. The man should not be the boss! I always put Nellie first.

Before Nellie met me, she never played cards or anything like that at all. I taught her to play Bridge and Mahjong. I was a very good bridge player. She learned so well and so fast that she became my partner every time we played and we always beat everybody! She learned the game and showed she had a brain! She conquered that game too. We had the envy of married couples.

I always told Nell, when people we know are getting a divorce. Don't take sides. Don't believe this one and that one. Just watch it and let it go. I told her, stay out of it.

The only regret I had was that I wasn't 6 ft tall, but Nellie made me feel like I was 6 feet tall! She always bought nice things for me and she would say, "You deserve it. You deserve it."

When I was courting Nell, that first week of June 1946, I thought about telling her about the incident with the fish and me and my mother. I did mention the incident, and Nellie never said a word, but I could see her eyes showing me sympathy. During the 74 years of our marriage, (Nellie being Japanese loved fish,) she never the mentioned the word fish to me or attempt to cook fish in our household. Whenever we would go out to eat, I would look for a restaurant that would serve fish. I watched her smile that looked as if it went around the world. She so enjoyed that fish, (trout was her favorite fish,) and it brought me joy to watch her enjoy it. I was so proud that she never asked me to be able to make fish. That's my Nellie. That's the kind of person she is. That fish dinner was a climax of a wonderful marriage.

CHAPTER SIX

ONE TIME WHEN WE WERE VISITING ERNIE BORGNINE at his house, his wife came down and she'd become "Beverly Hills." She was beautiful, and had slimmed down considerably. One night he was making a movie but told his wife to take us to a very expensive restaurant. She said, "Lou, you take care of the tipping." I thought, "Oh my goodness, in a place like this?" Thank heavens I had the cash on me, but we were visiting from Seattle. That's the way she was. She was very Beverly Hills. She would drive around in a fur coat in the summer. She only married him because he was a "Borgnine". She became a very rich woman because of her ambition. She invited us at Ernie's urging to his 80th birthday party at the

Beverly Hills Hotel. We were part of the group, but we were nobodies. Anthony Quinn was there, Les Brown, and other famous people. It was a black-tie affair, but I didn't have a black suit. Nellie bought me a new suit but we got to the party and I was the only one in a black suit. I could've been a waiter! I could've passed out drinks and collected tips.

And during our lifetime, which is still existing, because of Nellie, we met Mr. Grudd, who helped us to buy our house, expecting nothing in return. We met Ernest Borgnine through Nellie, and we became a very good friends for over 50 years. He treated us so well and asked for nothing. Then she met Rosemary LaPlanche. At every place I ever work at, she was the belle; the belle of the ball. People took to her. They gravitated to her. When we went to her high school reunions in Visalia, the men would say, "Oh, here's Hot Sumi!" I wasn't jealous. I was proud. They just all loved her. Oh, what a wonderful life we were having. I always say, "I wish I had a wish." Nellie has given me the most fabulous life I can dream of and everything she did was for me and everything I did was for her. That's the way I feel. All the people she caused to be our friends, who were the most kind people to us. It was because of Nellie, not me. She always made sure we ate the right things, and had the right diet. That's why we're heading to 98 years old. Men are too stupid to appreciate the wife they have. Men forget too quickly about the promises they've made. You should never forget your wife. I don't think I would be alive today if it wasn't for Nellie. We're both going to be 98 years old this year. It's due to her quiet handling of me. She always spoke in such a gentle way, guiding and directing. Not pushing. She was always proud of me.

Nellie has been, still is and will always be the greatest wife on earth. I didn't demand anything but she did the laundry, was my tailor, sewed the French cuffs on my shirts, hemmed my trousers, fed me. Her food was intelligent and tasty has brought us to our 98th birthdays this year, in 2020. That's what I call, not just a husband and wife, but a good partnership. A partnership of equal terms with neither being superior to the other. We listened to each other's counsel.

A while back, maybe 15-20 years ago, Nellie invited two of her friends, from way, way back. They were a Japanese couple who lived in Los Angeles. Nellie and these people were with each other in the concentration camps during the war. They were in their teens and were good friends. Nellie had not seen them since the 1950s. I have no idea how they got in touch with each other. Well, Nellie invited them over for dinner but did not mention it to me. After dinner, while we sat there drinking our after-dinner coffee. The woman asked if I was an aviation cadet. It startled me because no one knew that about me. I was so shocked. It seems that her neighbor in Buena Park knew an aviation cadet, named Moore in San Antonio. I said, "Yeah, that's got to be me." It was most unusual because I was the only Chinese man in the world with the last name of Moore. She said, "She said, you got along just fine." I asked her to follow me to the hallway in the apartment where Nellie had a gallery of pictures and I showed her the picture of me as a cadet. I couldn't believe that we had that connection, that a woman I knew, knew this woman. I said, "I'd like for you to arrange a meeting with her." I couldn't sleep that night. I kept thinking about it, and kept thinking about it.

The lady eventually called back and said, "She doesn't want to meet you." I was so shocked. I truly wanted to meet her, but I wanted Nellie to know that this was something from the past and not to worry about it to assure her that there was nothing to it. I couldn't believe she didn't want to meet after such a remarkable connection. I couldn't persuade the situation, but this lady wouldn't move. I could only surmise one of two things: either her husband was a strict Japanese man who didn't want her to meet a former boyfriend, or maybe she's out of shape and doesn't want me to see that lady of today with the today of 1942. That ended that.

Nellie was very kind and generous throughout this whole story, but I can imagine there was some feeling. I let the whole matter drop as I could see the reunion wasn't going to happen. I knew not meeting would not affect my life at all.

I would like my dear readers to know that when you get married, you are declared "man and wife," but you are not man and wife. You are partners. We are equal partners. We share everything. We share our thoughts and are able to finish each other's sentences. A partnership is based on equal values. You have to be in love, and tolerant. You have to worship that person. Never is there an ill thought or obscene thought between the two. That's what to me, marriage. Is. It is not over after the honeymoon, or after the first child is born. Sometimes after a child is born, the mother is stuck at home with the baby and the baby is the only thing she can talk to. The man can go to work and have lunch with buddies and even stop for a drink on the way home. But, there was none of that between Nellie and me. I recognized that Nellie was all alone during my working hours. I always made it a point to talk about my day at the office and she was always interested to hear it. I would fill her in with things she could remember later on. Things that were interesting to her.

You must have humility; you must show that she's a human being. She can cry with tears with sadness or tears of glee and a smile on her face that she always has ready for you when you arrive home from work. I preach this to many men, but you'd be surprised how many men are not interested. So many men don't recognize that the woman they marry is a human being and has to share in your life. Share you day, or talk about the politics in the country. Nellie and I agreed on everything. When you get home from work, say something soft and kiss her cheek. Say something tender in her ear. Even when I was at work, I'd call her five times just to say hello. She was always on my mind. I knew I was always on her mind. All of the little things she did for me, cooked for me, decorated, etc. told me how much she thought of me. Every man should cherish his life with his wife. He should give a soft touch of her hand. Even at 70, 80 or 90 years old.

I always entered the house with a big smile and a big kiss. I loved it tremendously. Nellie is fabulous. That's what I believe a marriage should be... compassion, devotion, tolerance, honesty, and deeply in love. Still, after 70 years of marriage. I'm still in as much love as I was in 1946. It's not a show. It comes from the heart. That, dear readers, is what I call eternal love.

We had some hardships. We had some medical problems, each of us. One time, when I had my gallbladder removed and I was in the hospital. I opened my eyes and saw a picture of the two of us there in the operating room. When she was in the hospital, I stayed in her room. When you are in the hospital, it is the most devastating fear of your life. They don't take that good care of you. We would give each other hope.

When the doctor told me that I was going into the hospital because I had pneumonia, I feared that I would die in the hospital. They didn't work to lift my morale and I wish everyone to work more to lift other's morale. When you work in health care, your first job should be to give others a life. Your voice has to carry a smile. Nellie always had a smile and a cheerful face for me.

I was once interviewed for a job with TRW, one of the biggest businesses in the country a while ago. The gentleman interviewing me asked me questions and stopped and asked, "Do you have any faults?" I said, "I would be stupid if I told you!" He said, "Hey, that's a good answer!" and he wrote this down.

I used to give lectures at the local high school. I did it off the top of my head. I did these things because I desired to help other people. I've always wanted to help other people. That's been my whole purpose. Every job I had involved people. Every project I took on helped people. I wanted to help give people a stronger a hand in life. Everything is from my heart. I've written stories from my life and they are from my heart.

At times at work, I had to go out of town for a week or so. I always left Nellie with sushi and she loved it. One time, I had to go with a Japanese man from Chicago. As soon as we sat down for dinner, I said, "Excuse me," and I left to go call my wife. He was so surprised that I called my wife, even though I saw her that morning. The next morning, I put cards in the mail for her and he was so surprised by that. I did it because I wanted her to know that I loved her and that I was with her, even when I was away. He was so shocked that I would do this. I saw his culture. They didn't care about their wives. At the end of the workday, they'd go to a bar and buy a bottle of scotch and listen to other girls sing. I preferred to be home and with Nellie. That was the most important thing to me.

When I would go out of town locally, Nellie would go with me and bring our dog. Sometimes Nellie would join me when I would speak. I always looked over at her and saw her smile. That gave me the strength and courage to go on.

Nellie's father was a typical old, Japanese man. Her mother was the glue that held the family together. When Nellie and I arrived in California, we lived in a rented house in back of another house. There was no refrigerator, only an icebox. Her mother came over and saw that and two days later a truck came and delivered a new refrigerator. Her mother worked for 90 cents an hour at a chicken factory, plucking feathers. Later, they delivered a washing machine. Here mother put it on credit and paid it off for us. I always appreciated her mother very, very much. We took care of her as best we could over the years. We once took her to dinner. She had never been to an American restaurant. We took her to the Velvet Turtle. She was shocked at the prices and didn't want me to spend the money. Every time we visited her, Nellie would bring a sweater, or shoes or something she bought for her mother. Her mother would always make me a Japanese dish of noodle soup that she knew I loved. That was her way of saying, "I love you." She only knew a couple words of English.

Nellie's mother passed while we were living in Washington. We felt so badly about it, but there was nothing we could do about it. He mother came up to Washington and showed our employees how to cut large shrimp for butterfly shrimp. We had the largest best, beautifully cut butterfly shrimp like no one else.

Nellie's mother loved our dog. She and our dog became the closest of buddies. At night, our dog stayed with her the whole time she stayed with us in Washington. She didn't know any English, but she knew how to handle the wholesalers that bought produce from their farm. Nellie learned from her. For that, I thank her mother. Her mother was a very charming lady. She treated me like a son, rather than a son-in-law. I treated her better than I did for my mother. Whatever, we bought her, she would put in a trunk and would never wear them, as if they were too nice to wear and she wanted to save it for something special. We would typically visit and take her to the movies in Little Tokyo. I would always leave her some money on the table. One time I left a rather large bill but she wanted to give it back to me and didn't want to accept it, but I told her I wanted her to have it.

Another aspect of a good marriage. Be grateful. Be appreciative. I always said, "That was a nice dinner." It only takes a word or two to give someone a nice lift. It's a simple thing.

I'm a very forward person. I don't say things to hurt people. I say things to help people.

Nellie gave me the courage to take on and tackle. I couldn't have done it without her support.

Nellie helped make that restaurant because she was in charge of the dining room and the girls.

I bought a short Japanese gown and a Chinese skullcap. Whenever I had a free moment, I would go around and entertain the tables with a large brass gong. I enjoyed bringing happiness to other people. That's my life. Nellie is my life. And I'm sure, I know, I am her life. A key is to give your partner hope.

I would help many Oriental people or others from Europe to help them write letters to fight against tickets. Most of them got out of their tickets or at least had them reduced. One time I helped a Korean family whose son was injured in a skiing accident at Bear mountain. I wrote a letter advocating for them, and the bill was reduced in half. The family was so grateful that they sent me beautiful new bed covers of satin. I did things like that for many people. Nellie makes me want to do good, considerate things for people. Nellie is in my mind when I do good things for other people. I always introduced Nellie in every one of my lectures.

I did something for the Cerebral Palsy Association.

They were making kitchen adaptations and I encouraged them to make things for kitchens. I found an apartment that needed help and I asked them to allow them to have them put in kitchens cabinets for them. I said, "Let's go bigger!" I got an apartment building of 75 units. The head of the cerebral palsy association was so shocked! It was a $100,000 job for them. I always go for the idea, "You can do it!" and I support them with my voice.

Our apartment building was robbed multiple times so I wanted to buy Nellie a gun. I called the police department and asked what kind of gun I should buy. They said they couldn't give me that information but then I asked what they would do for their wives---THEN THEY TOLD ME!

I deplore the term "my old lady". I resent it! That is your wife! Your partner! You should show more respect. That term doesn't show any love or respect. It's not fair to the woman. Of course, this whole book is about being fair and loving to your wife! I hate that expression. Over the last 20 years, people have always asked both Nellie and I why we don't have any wrinkles on our face and our neck. I would answer, "It's because we don't argue." If we have a disagreement, we talk it over. We sit on the couch, hold hands. I would turn to face her and listen to her problem to determine if I contributed to her problem or not. At any rate, we never argued. We always talked it over. When you don't argue, you don't have a scowl on your face or terror in your eyes. You show tenderness of love and devotion and a willingness to listen and share and possibly resolve the problem. You never raise your voice and you say each word with tenderness and devotion. You never get up and walk around a room angry. If worse comes to worse, you never go out and slam the door. No argument is worth the value of your marriage. NO ARGUMENT is worth the value of your marriage. When your discussion is concluded, wrap your arms around her shoulders, give her a kiss on her cheek and then on the lips and whisper in her ear, "I'm sorry. I was wrong and I love you." Get rid of the words "me" and "mine." Use the word, "ours." Your marriage should always offer to your wife, or loved one, your love:

- devotion
- faithfulness
- thoughtfulness
- tolerance
- understanding

- caring
- compassion
- listening
- patience
- togetherness

and a smile with each sound of your voice and a continuous demonstration of all the things above. Always express your love and always say, "I love you." Say it with tenderness and sincerity and demonstrate that the words, "I love you," are the most powerful words you can use to show your wife.

On June 10, the years 2010, Nellie and I celebrated our 64th wedding anniversary. We always wrote special notes to each other on that date. On that date, without fail, she would give me her letter first. On that date, I couldn't believe what I was reading. She remembered things from that first week that we were together that I didn't have any recollection of. She reminded me of a very flat joke that I told her. That joke was in her letter 64 years later! She remembered that we went to Baltimore so we wouldn't have to wait to get married. She never spoke of these things, but they we important to her; important enough to put into a letter 64 years later.

The letter expressed her joy that I proposed to her June 9th, 1946, when I held her hand and asked her to be my wife. She expressed her gratitude for the war, that because of the war, we met. Our love was so deep and full of compassion and full of devotion, full of togetherness and tenderness. She wrote these all these things. I had her open my letter to her, and I described exactly the same things she described. Our minds were one, which was our love for each other. It was such a wonderful feeling to know that she had kept all these feelings and memories in her heart all of these years. When we finished reading each other's letters, we shared tears of love and joy. They were the most wonderful tears you could ever expect to see. At the close of each letter, we each wished that we would have many, many more years of being happy and healthy together. Our minds were like one and nobody could tell us differently, even after 64 years we still held hands in the movies and walking to the grocery store. After 64 years, she would see things, and I would ask, "Do you like it?" Then, I would say "Merry Christmas." After 64 years, we still showed great passion and affection for each other. After 64 years, I still said, "I love you," every day. After 64 years, we NEVER embarrassed each other. We always looked after each other. Nellie was my monitor just in case I ever started to slide off the deep end. After 64 years, I would tell her how beautiful she looked and how well she kept her shape. After 64 years, we still say please and thank you. After 64 years, I still loved her deeply. Now we've been married for 74 years. And that dear readers, is what I consider Eternal Love.

I LOVE YOU!

AFTERWORD

And now, dear readers, I must tell you something very heartbreaking and very sad. On October 18, 2020, my dearest wife/partner, Nellie, passed away. It was the saddest day in my life. I cannot believe that she is gone, but I do believe that phase two of our Eternal Love begins, because I know that one day, I will reach up to the heavens, as far as I can, and Nellie will grab my hands and pull me up alongside her and we will kiss like we did in June of 1946. We will again enjoy each other, to touch each other, tenderly, and lovingly and whisper sweet words as we did for 74 years. It will be the greatest celebration of our lives to declare to each other, our love, devotion, compassion, thoughtfulness, togetherness, caring, trusting and making each other the happiest person on earth. I hope this time, it will be heaven. And so, I must draw this book to a conclusion. I've told you all about Nellie. This last entry, I have presented with tears of love for my dearest Nellie, who gave me the greatest 74 years of my life. I wish that all of the people in the world could experience the love that Nellie and I demonstrated for each other on a minute to minute basis. I hope that somewhere you will find a bit of Nellie and I in your life. We wish you well. That is the essence of the title of this book, Eternal Love.

Goodnight, Nellie.

In this photo, Nellie is the second girl from the right.

*On that fateful night when Lou first saw Nellie perform,
her position was third from the right. In this photo, only eight chorus
line girls are shown, but that night ten chorus line girls performed.*

ACKNOWLEDGMENTS

No matter what, Love finds a way.

Stacy Alvey, Lou's good neighbor and a mental health professional, believed in Lou's powerful story and lovingly typed every word as it was spoken by Lou. She transformed family photos into digital images and arranged them as illustrations in the book.

Mike Burroughs, owner of the Broken Bit Steakhouse, felt compelled to introduce Lou to Dennis, a trusted journalist who could share Lou's extraordinary story with a community who cares deeply about veterans.

Dennis Anderson, journalist and veterans advocate, wrote about Lou for a Veteran's Day feature in the local newspaper and then introduced Lou and his manuscript to his longtime friend Robin, a book publicist and coach.

Robin Blakely, CEO of Creative Center of America, organized a team of passionate creatives to publish Lou's book and worked with Lou, Stacy, and Dennis to creatively direct the project and fast-track publication.

Melanie Geiss edited the book for punctuation and managed all the publishing platform details to bring the work to market.

Garrett Stroginis created the interior design and formatting of the e-book and hardcover editions of the book.

Tracy Lynn, owner of Virtually Possible Designs, worked diligently to create the extraordinary dust jacket to reflect the beauty of the love story.

As a way to honor an American veteran, as a way to preserve the rare voice speaking authentically about the Asian American experience from World War II, as a tangible way to make the dream of writing a book by a 98-year-old man come true ... this book was lovingly created as a lasting tribute with genuine love and deep respect for Nellie and Lou.

A SPECIAL VETERAN'S DAY TRIBUTE TO LOUIS MOORE

Lou at the Broken Bit Steakhouse in Lancaster, CA during his interview with Dennis Anderson.

MOORE RETURNS FROM WAR TO FIND TRUE LOVE

By Dennis Anderson

November 11, 2020

QUARTZ HILL — Sitting in a local steak house, Lou Moore, who is 98 years old, wears his "World War II Veteran" ball cap at a rakish angle and makes his mission statement, "Time is of the essence."

For anyone nearing the century mark, that is a self-authenticating statement. For Moore, the mission statement is about telling his life story with the love of his life.

First, because today is Veterans Day, the day when we honor all who have served, it is worth reviewing a bit about his service during history's greatest conflict. It has its ups and downs.

"I volunteered to fly, as an aviation cadet," Moore recalled.

There was a room with a couple of hundred applicants and when they were done, only 35 were left, and they advanced to the next stage of training.

For Moore, it was an open cockpit plane, the kind where you sat on the parachute.

A training accident and mishap meant that he would be pulling ground duty for the rest of the war, but off he went to the European Theater of Operations. Attaining the rank of staff sergeant, he served as airfield security in England and after the D-Day invasion in France and into Germany.

"Dirt airfields, you know, out in the fields," Moore recalled.

And that was how it was. The tactical air forces — ground attack aircraft like P-47 Thunderbolts, P-38 Lightnings and such, got moved onto roughly improved air fields while the Allies were advancing to beat the Nazis.

So, Moore did his part. He remembers being in a French village near the German border, sitting down at a bistro and a local Frenchman, recently liberated, liberated him of 19 of his 20 cigarettes.

But that is not what he remembers most about the great World War II. Moore remembers his wife Nellie, who passed on Oct. 18 — she was also 98. She was the greatest victory that Moore experienced from returning home from World War II.

It was not easy to be a Chinese-American member of the US armed forces in World War II. It was even less easy to be Japanese-American, a Nisei. But Moore and his bride-to-be formed a uniquely American alliance out of the end of World War II.

"I was the only 'Oriental' in any unit I served in," Moore recalled. "My name is Moore. I am third-generation Chinese-American, but when my grandfather arrived in America, the official with the badge could not pronounce his name, so he told him his name was Moore."

He recalls the prejudice he experienced in the armed forces, particularly at the hands of a bigoted officer, but that he withstood the verbal abuse and "sing-song" English with stoicism because there was nothing to be done about it.

"I would have liked to kill him, but where would that leave me?" Moore asked. "So, I ignored it. I never talk about the war."

Homecoming, and his life-long love, is what he talks about. He has put so much thought into the subject that he wrote a short volume titled "Eternal Love" and it is dedicated to Nellie, to whom he was married for 74 years.

Moore's family settled in Brooklyn and the retired businessman still has traces of a Brooklyn accent. Almost as soon as he returned home, his family urged that they go visit a new night club in Manhattan, The China Doll, on 47th Street between 7th Avenue and Broadway.

Mike Burroughs, owner of the Broken Bit Steakhouse in Quartz Hill, always has an eye out for veterans and supports veteran causes, like the local nonprofit, Vets4Veterans. He spotted Moore's ball cap, "World War II Veteran" and became acquainted.

"He's a great American," Burroughs said.

Moore remembers that outing to the China Doll night club in 1946 like it was yesterday. The trip and the chorus line gave him his first glimpse of Nellie. She was third from the end in the chorus line and she was the only one he had eyes for.

If Moore had experienced some of the prejudice common in his day and that time in America, what Nellie experienced was infinitely worse. As a

Japanese-American, she had been interned during the war panic that swept the United States after Japan's surprise attack on Pearl Harbor on Dec. 7, 1941.

She was from Visalia, Calif. and all Americans of Japanese ancestry on, or near the West Coast, were rounded up and put into relocation centers, that Moore says, in reality, were concentration camps.

No American of Japanese ancestry was ever tried or convicted of any act against the United States during World War II.

But by the time Lou and Nellie Moore met, the war was over. Their first meeting was over coffee at an Automat near the night club. That was on June 1, 1946. They spent days talking to one another. By June 10, they were married.

"We took the train to Baltimore, because in Baltimore you did not have to wait to get married like in New York," Moore said.

He went on to a successful career in management consulting, philanthropy and in volunteering with disadvantaged students. Along the way, Nellie was his support, his counselor, sometimes his mentor and always his partner.

In his book, "Eternal Love," he wrote, "That's what I call not just a husband and wife, but a good partnership. A partnership of equal terms, with neither being superior to the other. We listened to each others counsel."

And they had such adventures. They left New York to return to California. For a while, they lived in Washington state. Along the way, they started and ran restaurants and he helped businesses grow and she took on jobs in which she succeeded. They did not grow a family together, but they continued to grow as a couple. They had a decades-long friendship with the Academy Award-winning actor Ernest Borgnine. They made many friends and out of rough beginnings, they prospered and enjoyed a long life and marriage together.

"That is why I call it 'Eternal Love,'" he said of the volume he wrote in praise of a lifetime lived with Nellie – two people who never gave up on each other, and who never gave up on America."

Losing Nellie in this life, he said, has been "heartbreaking, and very sad … the saddest day in my life. I cannot believe that she is gone, but I do believe that phase two of our eternal love begins, because I know that one day, I will reach up to the heavens, as far as I can, and Nellie will grab my hands and pull me up alongside her, and we will kiss like we did in June of 1946."

To learn more about Nellie & Lou, please visit
www.CreativeCenterOfAmerica.com/Lou